FAMOUS BANJO PICKIN' TUNES

by Janet Davis

www.melbay.com/98530BCDEB Online A

Visit us on the Web at www.melbay.com – E-mail us at email@

TURKEY IN THE STRAW
MELODIC – STYLE

G TUNING - KEY OF D   **OPTIONAL: RETUNE 5TH STRING TO A**

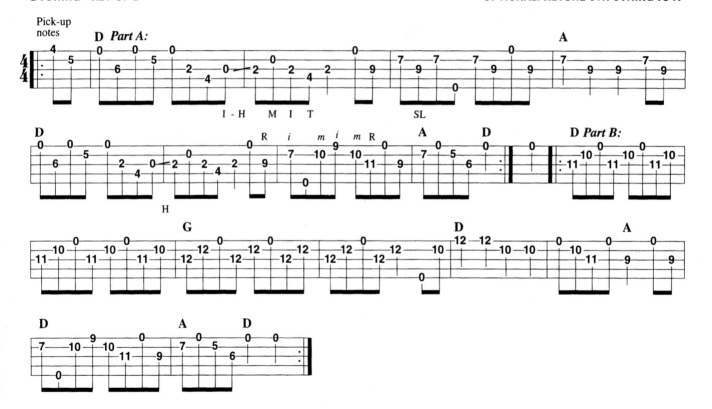

AULD LANG SYNE

Should old acquaintance be forgot? A traditional Scottish tune, first put on paper in 1788
by Robert Burns who heard it sung by an old man.

G TUNING - KEY OF G

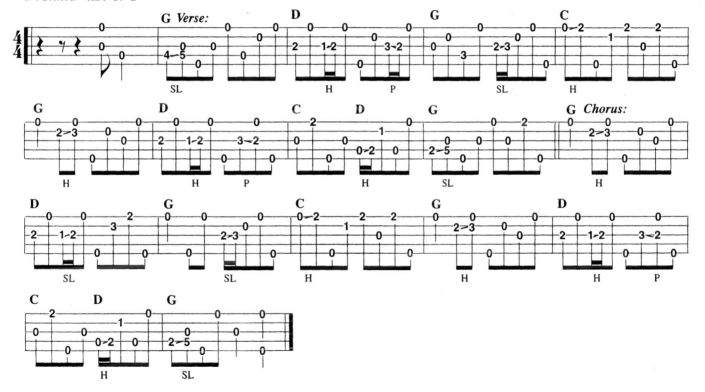

THE EIGHTH OF JANUARY

This popular fiddle tune has been the basis for other famous songs and soundtracks.

G TUNING - KEY OF D

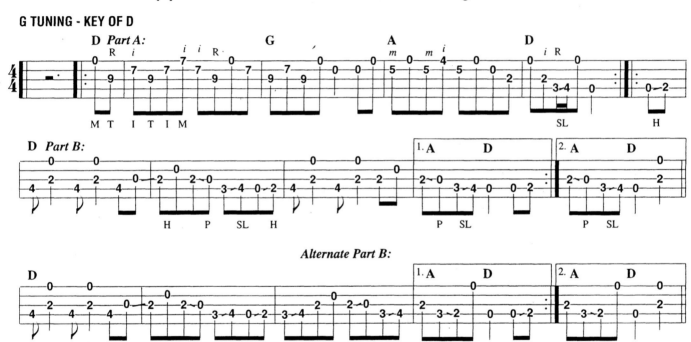

SWANEE RIVER
(THE OLD FOLKS AT HOME)

Written by Stephen Foster in 1851.

G TUNING - KEY OF G

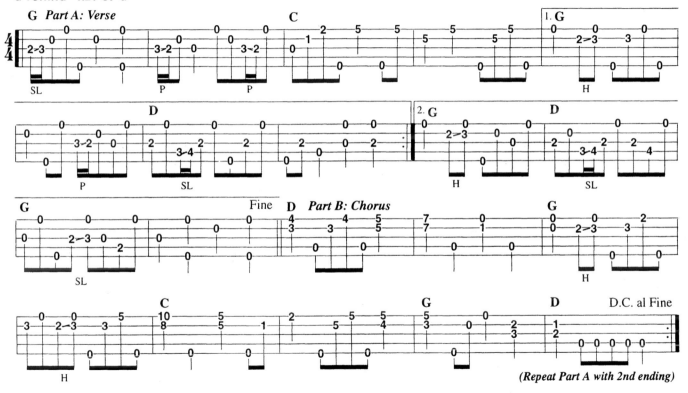

(Repeat Part A with 2nd ending)

OLD SPINNING WHEEL

G TUNING - KEY OF C
CAPO 2ND FOR KEY OF D

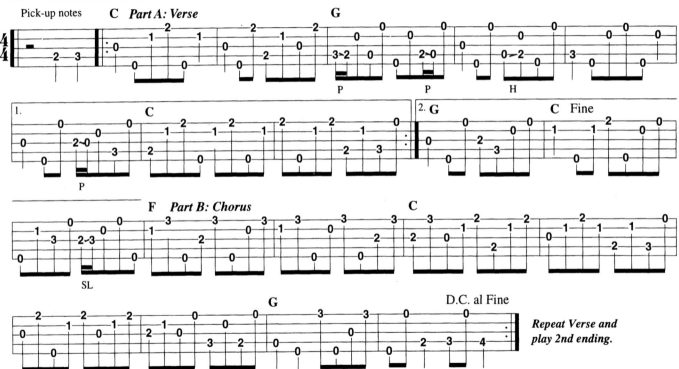

Repeat Verse and play 2nd ending.

OH, SUSANNA

The first major hit by composer Stephen Collins Foster in the mid 1850s.

G TUNING - KEY OF G

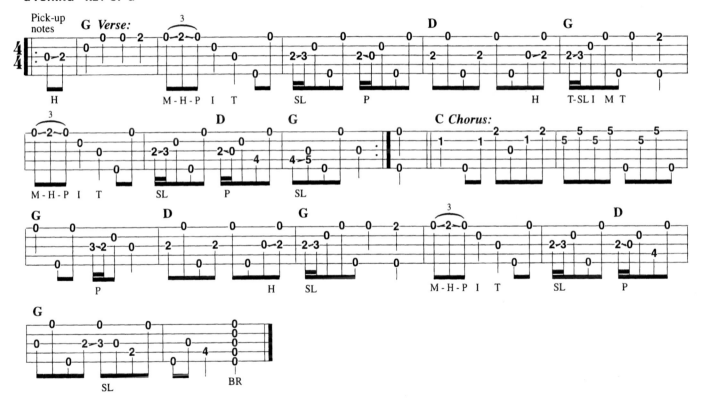

HOUSE OF THE RISING SUN

This bluesy tune about a house in New Orleans is usually sung in 3/4 time. Playing the lead on the banjo in 4/4 time adds a driving bluegrass effect. It can be played at the tempo of your choice.

G TUNING - KEY OF A MINOR - RETUNE 5TH STRING TO A

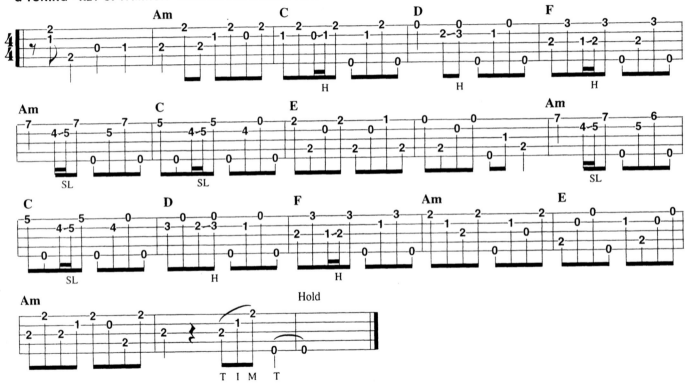

LA CUCARACHA

This popular and lyrical Mexican folk song is about a cockroach.

G TUNING - KEY OF C

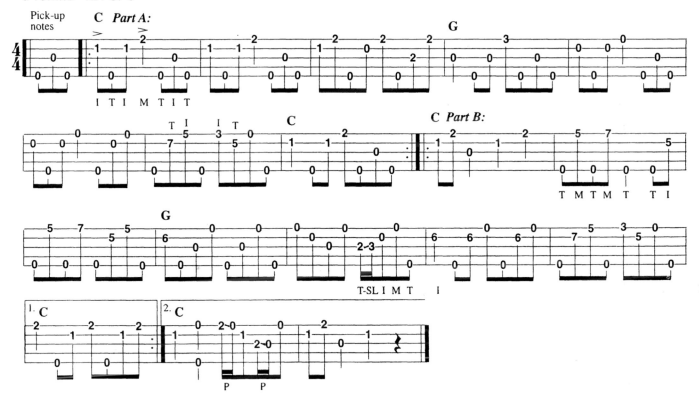

JUST A CLOSER WALK WITH THEE
TRIPLET STYLE

G TUNING - KEY OF G

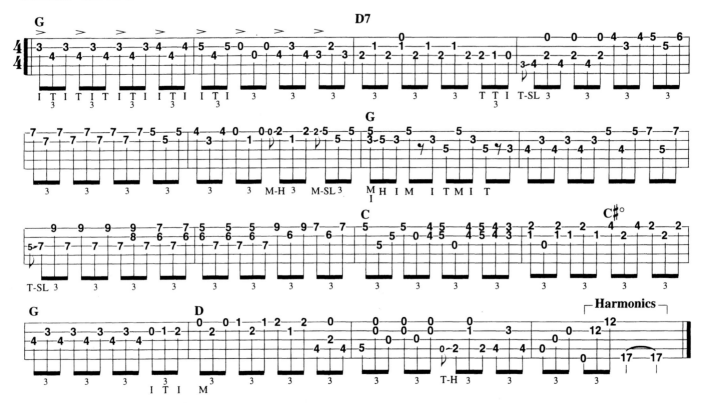

TOM DULA

A ballad originating in the late 1860s about the hanging of Tom Dula for murder, this tune was popularized by Gilliam B. Grayson in the 1920s and assured its place in musical fame by the recordings of Kingston Trio in the late 1950s.

G TUNING - KEY OF G

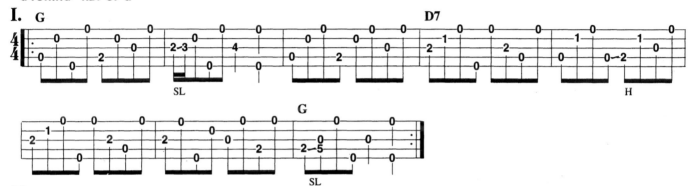

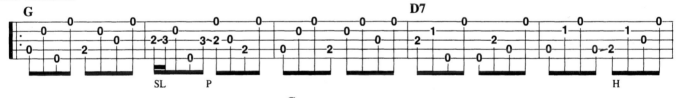

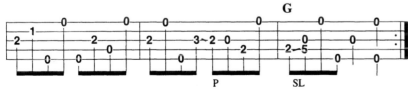

SWING LOW, SWEET CHARIOT

G TUNING - KEY OF G

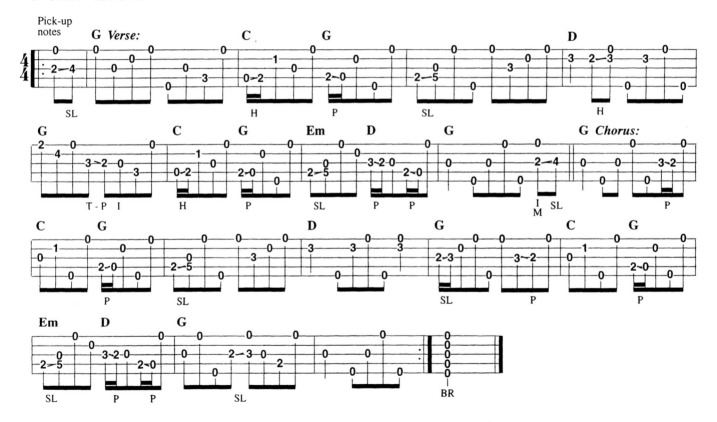

LITTLE BROWN JUG

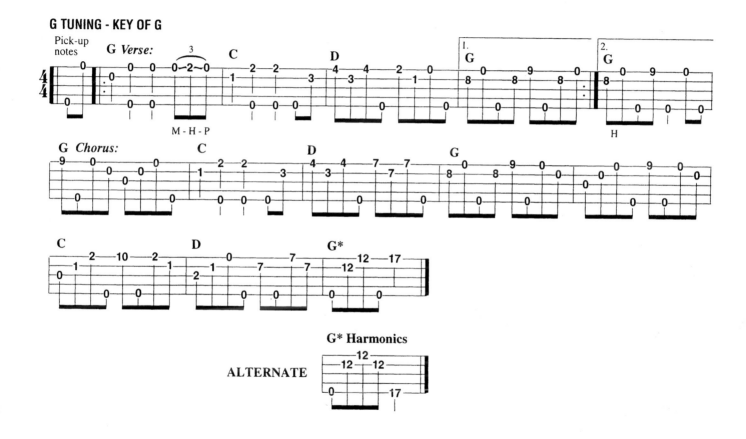

STAR SPANGLED BANNER (continued)

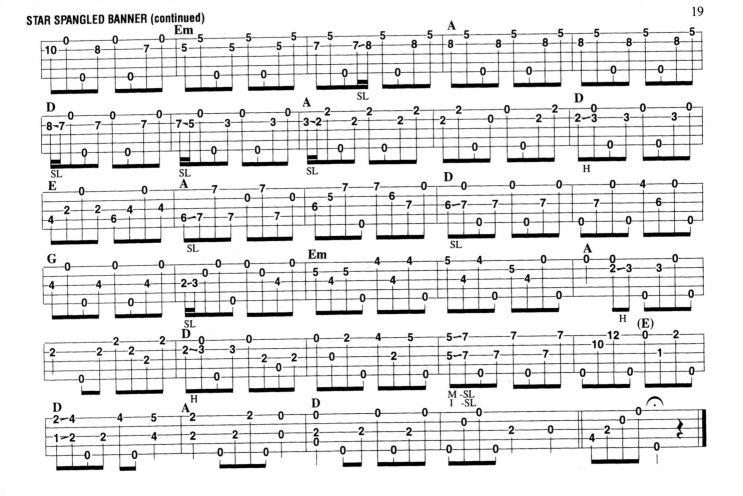

TWINKLE, TWINKLE LITTLE STAR

This is also the tune for the popular *Alphabet Song*...A, B, C, D, E, F, G...etc.

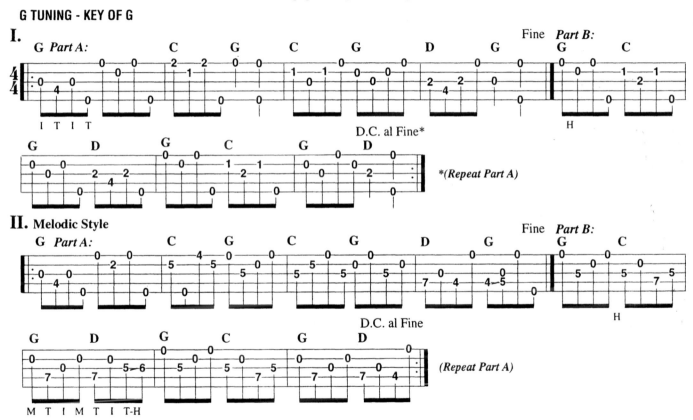

SKIP TO MY LOU

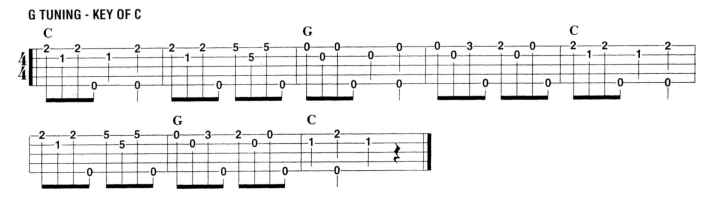

YANKEE DOODLE – DIXIE
A DUET: Playing both tunes at the same time!

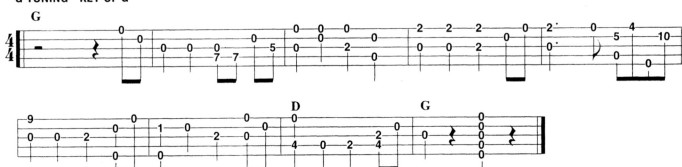

WILLIAM TELL OVERTURE

The overture for the opera Guillaume Tell, which was written by Rossini and produced in 1829, is often recognized as a theme song associated with various radio, television and motion pictures.

G TUNING - KEY OF C (CAPO 5TH FRET FOR KEY OF F)

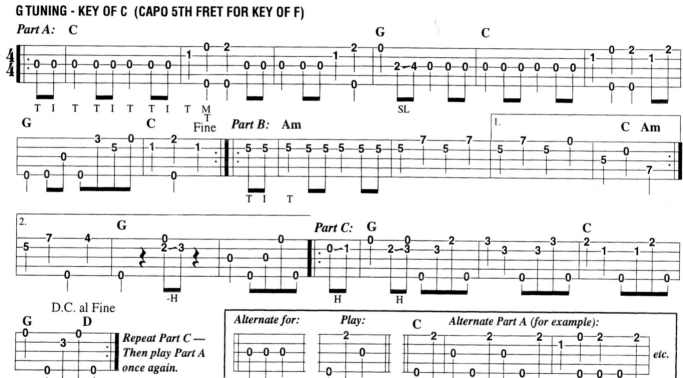

STAR SPANGLED BANNER
BLUEGRASS – STYLE

G TUNING - KEY OF D
RETUNE 5TH STRING TO A
CAPO 3RD FOR KEY OF F

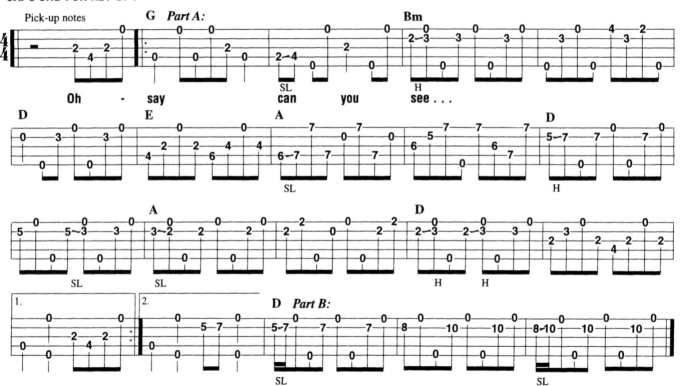

CHOP STICKS

Few people who have ever been around a piano, have missed hearing this tune.
It also makes an entertaining banjo tune! Try working out your own variations for this tune.

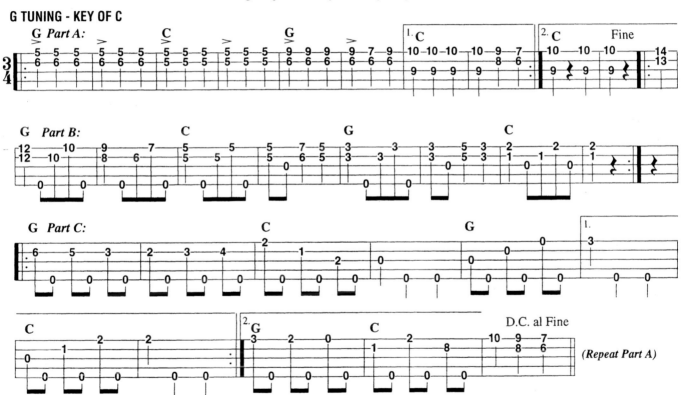

(Repeat Part A)

AMAZING GRACE
3/4 TIME

G TUNING - KEY OF G

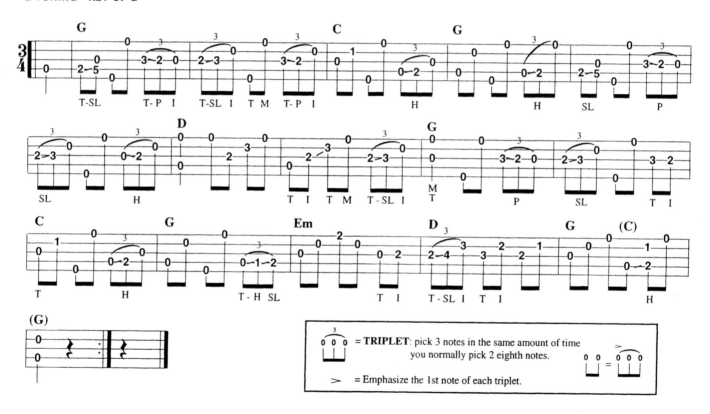

BEAUTIFUL BROWN EYES

WALTZ TIME (3/4) has 6 eighth notes per measure instead of the usual 8 eighth notes in 4/4 time.
Emphasize the first note of each measure to bring out the melody

G TUNING - KEY OF G

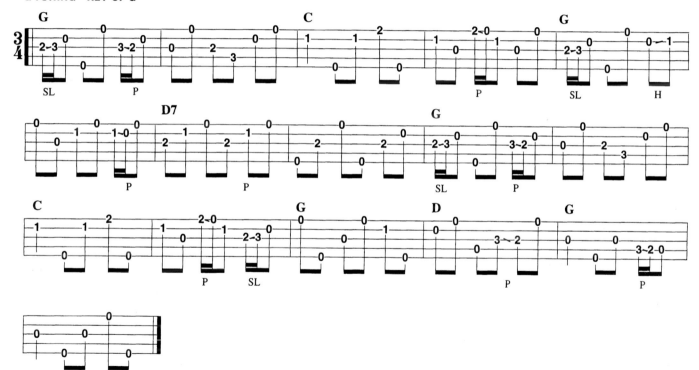

OH, WHEN THE SAINTS GO MARCHING IN

A favorite Negro spiritual, a popular tune for jazz improvisation in New Orleans style, and
a great bluegrass banjo tune!

G TUNING - KEY OF G

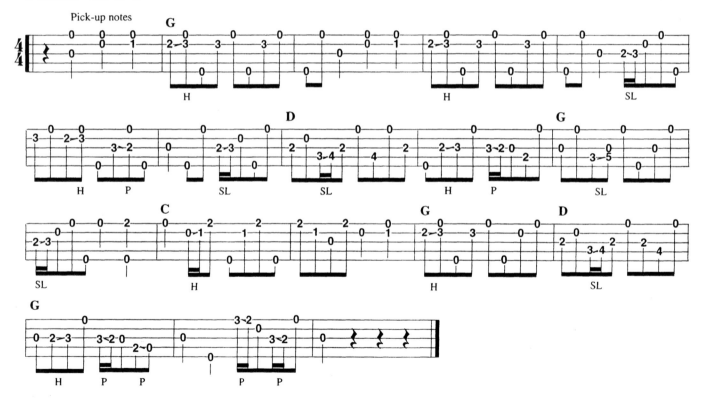

WABASH CANNONBALL

A popular tune often performed by country, folk, and bluegrass musicians.

G TUNING - KEY OF C

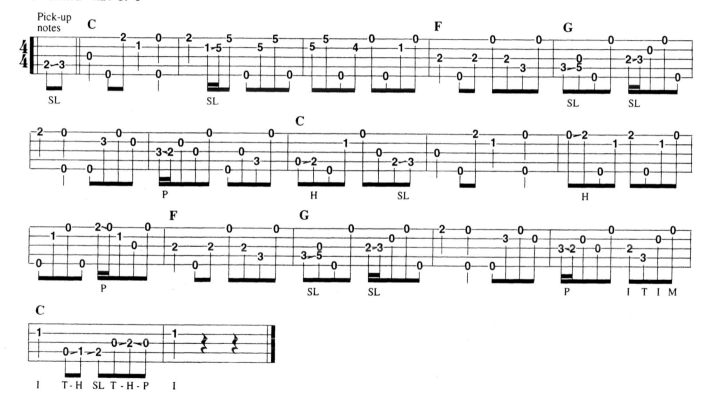

I'LL FLY AWAY

This well known gospel tune is arranged below using the Gm pentatonic scale, giving the tune a modal effect often used in the old Appalachian music. To play it with a standard G major "sound," change the 3s to 4s on the 1st, 3rd & 4th strings in the tablature.

G TUNING

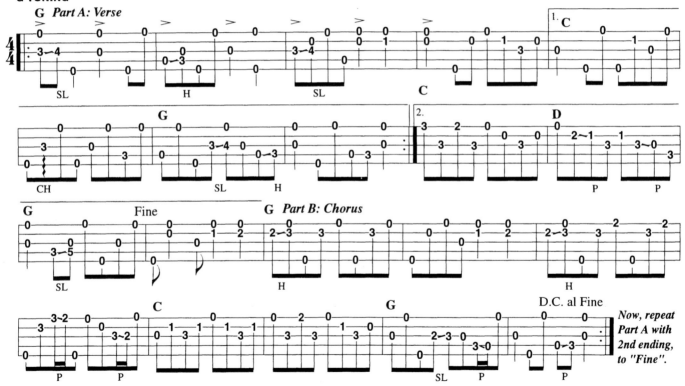

Now, repeat Part A with 2nd ending, to "Fine".

THE YELLOW ROSE OF TEXAS

Popular as a Confederate marching song, it later became a favorite for the Northern minstrel stages.

G TUNING - KEY OF C

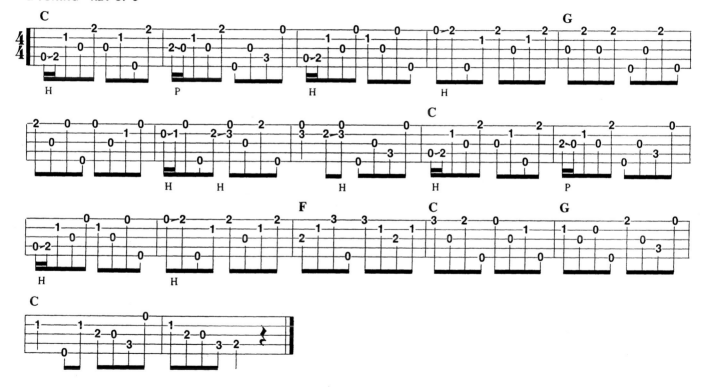

I'VE BEEN WORKING ON THE RAILROAD

G TUNING - KEY OF G

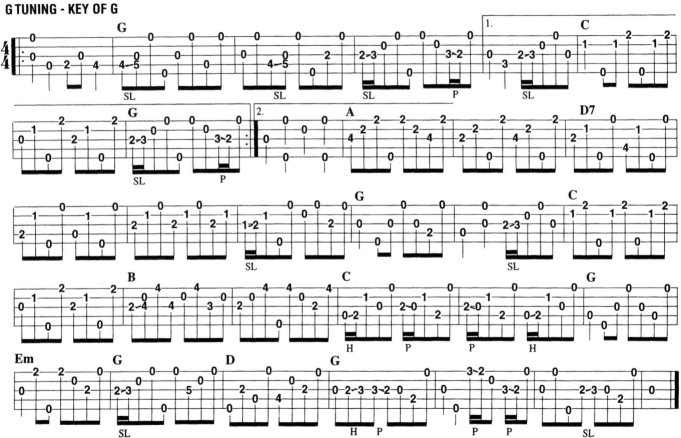

CAMPTOWN RACES

A Stephen C. Foster tune, written between 1850-1860, was very popular during the Civil War.

G TUNING - KEY OF G (CAPO 2ND FOR KEY OF A)

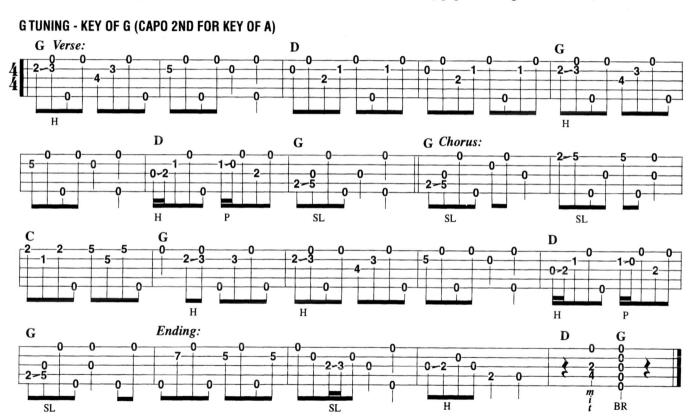

WHEN YOU AND I WERE YOUNG, MAGGIE

G TUNING - KEY OF G (CAPO 2ND FOR KEY OF A)

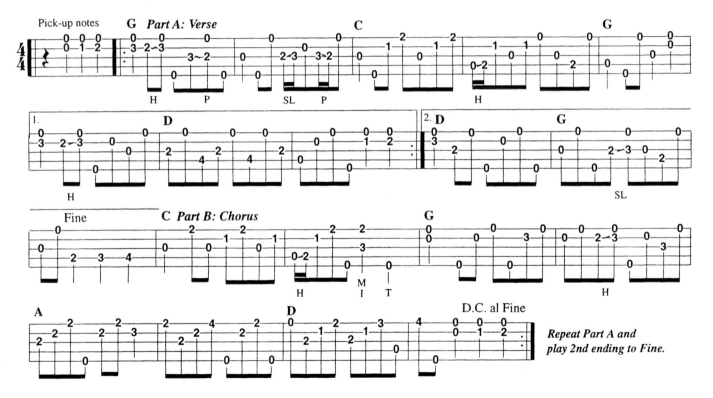

Repeat Part A and play 2nd ending to Fine.

SOMEONE'S IN THE KITCHEN WITH DINAH

Strumming on the Old Banjo

G TUNING - KEY OF G

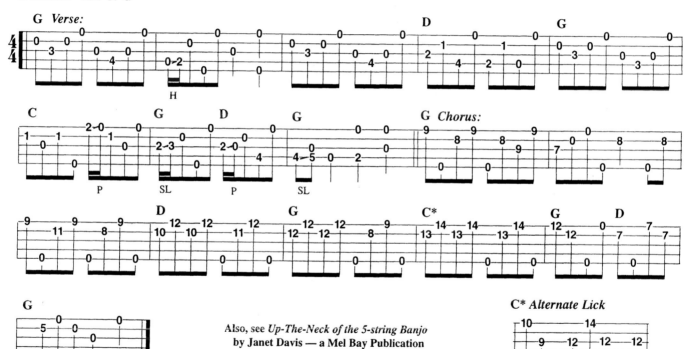

Also, see *Up-The-Neck of the 5-string Banjo*
by Janet Davis — a Mel Bay Publication

ARKANSAS TRAVELER
MELODIC – STYLE

G TUNING - KEY OF D

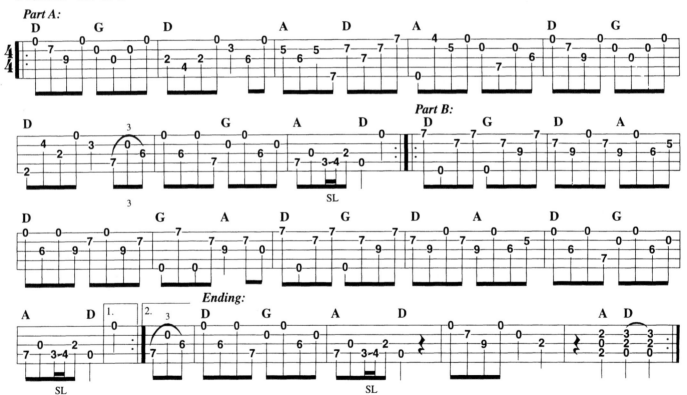

CONTENTS

NOTE Many famous tunes have two parts, Part A and Part B. If you see these symbols: [1.] [2.], use the 1st ending; then repeat the same section but play the 2nd ending. Then continue with Part B.

JINGLE BELLS

A popular bluegrass Christmas tune, this can be played with or without the harmonics.
(To play without the harmonics, just play the notes indicated in the tablature)

G TUNING - KEY OF G

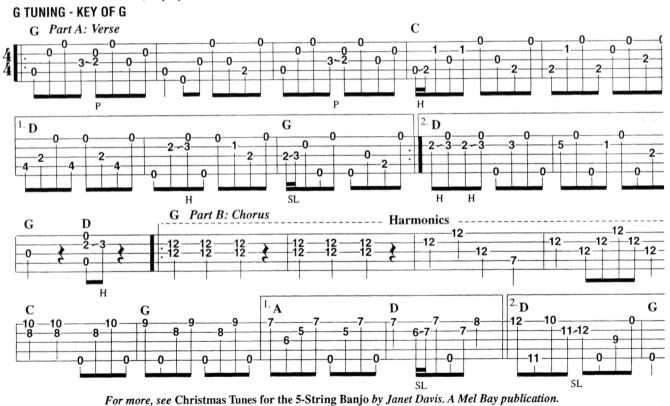

For more, see **Christmas Tunes for the 5-String Banjo** *by Janet Davis. A Mel Bay publication.*